LeadershipBites

Success Mindset in
Business and Entrepreneurship
(Volume one)

Alfred Oladapo

TABLE OF CONTENT

Introduction

There are basic concepts that shape entrepreneurial success in any place and at any time. These are very much operating in concentric circles.

These concepts are beyond just factors or parameters, they are existential to the many businesses that have transcended generations and remain very viable today.

The principles set in here are valuable to anyone who desires to operate a business successfully. A decision to ignore these may be an intention to chase an illusion that will soon fizzle into oblivion.

Before You Start

Neophyte Entrepreneurs will surely need all the help they can get to succeed. However, they must look for help in the right place if they will go far.

You cannot assume you have the ability for what you are trying to start or engage in any meaningful venture based on just what you "think" you can do.

An Entrepreneur that starts the journey with "bitterness", "unhealthy rivalry", "anger", "laziness", "frustrations", and a jaundiced understanding of what guarantees success should expect unpleasant surprises midway.

Entrepreneurs that commence the journey based on a wrong that was meted out to them in the past by someone or an organization in whom they may have invested trust, will lose unhindered access to ideas, reflect, meditate, and evaluate the framework for their decisions, and actions.

Connectivity begins with appropriate people skills, chief among the fundamentals is competency in self-respect communication, self-confidence, respect for boundaries, and the ability to discern the environment and read nonverbally.

No entrepreneur will create a resonance impact until s/he has learned the art of extensive preparation and intensive practice to attain some level of proficiency and quality skill.

It is inappropriate to engage in entrepreneurship until you are convinced that the foremost reason why you were employed in the organization you work for is that you are an outstanding person with the capacities and potential to start your own.

As all world-class athletes practice, and intensely prepare for competitions, to attain success; no entrepreneur will go far without submitting to excellent mentoring and coaching to gain the necessary skills!

Those who embrace entrepreneurship headlong are most likely not just going to make a huge success initially, they will also find fulfillment because they have chosen to quit helping other individuals build their dreams and vision.

Anyone who enters into the field of entrepreneurship without adequate preparation and training is most likely just investing in world-class "sinking sand".

Those who become entrepreneurs by choice are often
determined to invest in the best training that
guarantees success. But those who are forced to
"think" entrepreneurship are highly susceptible to
embracing the fire brigade mentality.

Successful Entrepreneurs are self-motivated individuals that are fully prepared for the long haul. They did not only believe they will succeed, but they also framed their minds that the journey was worth all the experiences; both pleasant and painful.

A resounding success in entrepreneurship is for those
who are fully prepared to join the league of those who
understand what it means to explore options through
lateral thinking. They have turned their backs on
vertical thinking.

Instead of getting involved in corrosive organizational politics, those who are baptized by entrepreneurial mentality spend a great deal of their time, energy, and resources preparing for their glorious exit from an organization they did not create and will not be given to them as a reward for their loyalty and hard work.

Nature and experience teach that when you operate in an enterprise you believe you were created for and in which you are thoroughly prepared to perform; then excellence is not far-fetched.

Those who desire to gain happiness and affluence tomorrow will see Entrepreneurs as a ready option and willingly take the bull by the horn and certainly resolve to pay the price today.

The Fundamentals

One clear advantage of having clarity before the commencement of the entrepreneurial experience is the ability to make a distinct choice between your brand identity and competition in the marketplace.

Entrepreneurial success thrives on an unmistakable
understanding of what you set out to do, what you
want to achieve, and above all, why you are doing
what you set out to do; that is the motive.

Clarity is the passion energy, events are the fuel for happiness. An unambiguous crystal clear answer to the "why" of your business will confidently establish if you can persevere in the face of hardships.

Entrepreneurs who readily embrace the "what", "why", and "how" of the business will readily avoid the traps and crises of finding and establishing an appropriate direction for the organization.

Undoubtedly, entrepreneurs who ignore the core fundamental questions will surely invite obscurity of ideas and incur avoidable emotional perturbations.

The inability to provide the right or workable answers to basic entrepreneurial questions will no doubt throw the business into boundless instability and make it vulnerable to trial and gross error.

The Limits of Financial Capital

Entrepreneurs' greatest resource is not finance, just as many people have been made to believe. The greatest resource any entrepreneur cannot do without is an "incisive mindset".

The cliché: "money drives entrepreneurial success" proceeds from vertical thinking which is an unfailing recipe for recurrent frustrations. An entrepreneurial journey that starts based on this perception is certainly dead on arrival!

If money is all that is required to start and run a business successfully, why do banks and other financial institutions who had humongous assets and huge financial resources in all kinds of currencies fail?

If you truly believe all you require to start your business and run it successfully is money, then how much money is enough to keep the business from unpredictable failure?

Great Entrepreneurs, who have become a success in
their chosen fields of endeavor, refused to buy into the
lie that money is all that is required to successfully
start and run a sustainable transgenerational business.

If money guarantees success in entrepreneurship, why are great businesses like airlines with huge fleets of expensive aircraft and other multinational companies with huge financial investments going down into the abyss daily?

Entrepreneurs that are in a hurry to make money eventually find the journey stressful and frustrating instead of exciting and adventurous because they rushed into a business with fragmented knowledge, half-baked knowledge, or outdated knowledge.

To assume that ability to make money in a business venture can make a person responsible is a great error. It takes self-discipline to become a disciplined person of worth in business.

Entrepreneurs that are hungry for success must accept
that many products' authenticity, durability, and value
for money are locked into the ability to deliver
excellent results in the shortest possible time.

Entrepreneurs who engage in systems thinking are at a great advantage for success and sustainability over those who start with a trial-and-error mentality and may eventually get carried away with simply making money.

Even when huge financial resources are available to an entrepreneur, the inability to engage the mind in creative imagination in all dimensions and fire from all cylinders may crystallize little chances of success.

Both established and entrepreneurial organizations have equal time; only 24 hours. Financial investments that ignore the cycle of timing are doomed to setbacks in their performance thereby affecting profits.

Except for an individual who has unlimited and unrestricted access to financial resources, one of the great qualities entrepreneurs must develop is the ability to improvise through creativity and innovation.

Great Entrepreneurs understand they are operating in a relationship flux. Consequently, they must continuously maintain healthy, emotional, psychological, financial, and physical balance within themselves and the outside world.

Unwillingness to make requisite sacrifices to grow the
organization combined with a disposition to build an
over-bloated staff at the beginning of a business will
put unnecessary pressure on the available financial
resources.

It amounts to a misplacement of priority when an Entrepreneur entirely focuses on how to raise financial capital ahead of acquiring the appropriate knowledge and skills required to build and sustain the business.

An entrepreneur who ignores investments to acquire crucial competencies upfront is treading on a highway leading to the valley of confusion where financial resources will be drained away at turbo-charged speed.

People whose minds are locked in the wrong reasons
for engaging in entrepreneurship will certainly begin
their journey with an extreme capital deficit; which
though cannot be redeemed by financial muscle, will
eventually erode the potential to equip their financial
vault.

Anyone strolling into entrepreneurship based on an undermining assumption that a strong financial muscle is all that it requires to begin a business and guarantee its success has surely bought a one-way ticket to the land of rude shock!

An entrepreneur that ignores acquiring appropriate skills in the design of the business will inevitably operate under a very tight financial budget, which then looks like skating on thin ice.

One of the great factors that often promote stability in the entrepreneurial expedition is the ability of the entrepreneur to embrace self-discipline in financial management.

Many entrepreneurs will do better when they have a rudimentary knowledge of accounting and bookkeeping. Failure to acquire these may accelerate the organization's descent into financial genocide.

Our intensive research on successful entrepreneurs reveals six major types of capital successful entrepreneurs possess. Though finance is one of them, the success of the business is not solely determined by its strong financial muscle.

People who deliberately destroy the financial fabric of the organization they are trusted to lead should not expect success in entrepreneurship if they funded the enterprise with the loot.

It is erroneous to assume when people talk about raising capital for business, it means they are simply referring to financial elasticity. So when people ask me how to raise capital to start their businesses my question is always: "what kind of capital"?

An entrepreneur that cannot keep an appropriate
record of financial transactions is a mobile accident
searching for where to happen ... even the man that
was given one talent kept a good record; at least he
returned the capital (one talent) intact.

Anyone who assumes entrepreneurial success is only hinged on strong financial muscle has not learned anything from the failure of great financial institutions and may expect shocking surprises ahead.

To deliberately begin a business you have passion for but lack the capacity and capability to drive is a calculated decision to embark on emotional, psychological, financial, and even spiritual suicide!

If techniques that will eventually prove too expensive
for the financial muscles and psychological fulfillment
in the business take initial priority, the enterprise will
face self-imposed challenges.

Interest starts to die pretty quickly once the parameters that trigger it are removed. When businesses simply start based solely on interest, the entrepreneur easily gives up in the face of intense competition in the marketplace, low productivity, average turnover, disappointment, unmet expectations, and huge financial deficits.

Since business is not charity and entrepreneurs require
finances to keep the product in the marketplace, the
business must be able to deal with the concept that the
product must be able to trigger a desire to attract
payment for it.

Those people with the mentality that "friends" are to sponsor their weddings, "parents and others" to finance the business they want to start, the "organization they work" to be solely responsible for their personal development, "Pastors" to always pay their rents, and the "church" to provide jobs for them may never become successful entrepreneurs.

The Mindset

Great entrepreneurs know the journey is not for lazy individuals who just want to lurk around and pry into another person's enterprise to form their product.

Entrepreneurs who will be highly successful must be willing to embrace change and be ready to jettison the mental disposition that enslaves their capacities and stifles their ability to deliver great results

Any deficit in the internal equilibrium of an entrepreneur will infect the organization with corrosive relationships of proportional dimensions that will spread like gangrene and poison the ambiance.

Persons who always have a catalog of individuals to blame for their misfortunes in business ... except themselves are comfortably lying to themselves!

An "incisive mind" is the engine room, powerhouse of ideas, and the center of entrepreneurial success. It is the factory that churns out creative ideas and intelligent innovations

When people approach entrepreneurship with a misaligned mindset that resonates between success and failure, it is almost inevitable that failure and frustrations become dependable allies in their harvest vault!

It is a delusion of high incomprehensibility to expect a leader's mindset that is locked in yesterday's outdated, out-modeled, fossilized, crude systems and structure to possess the capability, and capacity to excel in business.

Two crucial factors which intelligent Entrepreneurs cannot ignore in their quest to make a meaningful contribution to the economy are the condition of the environment and the mindset of the people.

Many people with entrepreneurial mindsets eventually never start because they got carried away with the good salary and allowances they presently enjoy and forgot that the real purpose of working in their present organization is to acquire relevant experience to kick-start their own.

Smart employers do not pay salaries out of their financial capital. So no matter how lucrative your salary may be right now; start making plans to become a great entrepreneur in the nearest future if you want lifelong financial freedom.

An organization that pays you a "good salary" now but stifles your creative ability, innovative capability, and critical thinking capacity is a "sweet" poison that is slowly eating away your future and corrosively eroding the foundation of your self-sustenance in your retirement.

Those whose resolve for entrepreneurship is not fully set before they start will speedily withdraw to the slavery of "earning salary" and subject themselves to the very insults, ridicule, abuse, dehumanization, frustrations, humiliation, and intimidation they rejected as initio when they encounter difficulties that test their tenacity.

An Entrepreneur that fails to relocate the mind from a regular job mentality has surely kept the exit door out of entrepreneurship perpetually open. It is only a matter of time before s/he beats a retreat from the world of uncertainty back to the world of a regular salary.

Persons with entrepreneurial mindsets in their present employment know they are simply helping to crystalize the vision and advance the dreams of others to the neglect of their future enterprise.

People who will succeed in entrepreneurship require a "no alternative mindset". They perceive their commitment to engage in entrepreneurship as a necessary bondage that they cannot break away from.

Those who begin the entrepreneurial voyage with a mindset of "maybe 1 will succeed, maybe it will work out, or let me just try" may have embraced monumental doubts and accommodated hidden failure in advance.

Entrepreneurial success is not built on a "try and error mindset". It is not a terrain for a perpetual apprenticeship mindset. It is not a place for those who want to just experiment. It is not a place to be entered into ill-advisedly.

A mindset that assumes a university certificate will guarantee a good job and regular meals is a product of jaundiced thinking, intellectual hollowness, and anti-entrepreneurship disposition.

A mindset that perceives a University degree in any field as a sure ticket to the good things in life is a guaranteed recipe for colossal disappointment and resounding frustration because such a mindset cannot explore the possibility of engaging in entrepreneurship.

An individual who deliberately or ignorantly chooses not to take his assignment with any seriousness but always prays for breakthroughs in business has chosen to embrace resounding misalignment and a blurred path to predictable disappointments and guaranteed failure.

Navigating Terrain of Failure

Successful entrepreneurs never started that business
with ambiguous or unclear directives because they
know it is near impossible to make appreciable
progress without clarity.

Everyone who starts a business based on unclear thinking is guaranteed to fail. That's why successful entrepreneurs deliberately refused to be trapped in average thinking and psychological derailment that creates jaundiced thinking.

As long as you believe you have an option of going back to paid employment, you are almost guaranteed to be a master showpiece in entrepreneurial failure.

Those who blatantly refuse to take responsibility for their lives but expect their organizations, bosses, husbands, wives, friends, neighbors, and government to bear the cost and the sacrifices prerequisite to their success have swallowed one of the greatest catalysts to entrepreneurial catastrophe.